THE
ABCs
OF
NONVIOLENCE

A
Spiritual
Perspective

Dean G. Van Wie

BALBOA.
PRESS

A DIVISION OF HAY HOUSE

Balboa Press books may be ordered through booksellers or by contacting:

Balboa Press
A Division of Hay House
1663 Liberty Drive
Bloomington, IN 47403
www.balboapress.com
1-(877) 407-4847

Because of the dynamic nature of the Internet, any web addresses or links contained in this book may have changed since publication and may no longer be valid. The views expressed in this work are solely those of the author and do not necessarily reflect the views of the publisher, and the publisher hereby disclaims any responsibility for them.

The author of this book does not dispense medical advice or prescribe the use of any technique as a form of treatment for physical, emotional, or medical problems without the advice of a physician, either directly or indirectly. The intent of the author is only to offer information of a general nature to help you in your quest for emotional and spiritual well-being. In the event you use any of the information in this book for yourself, which is your constitutional right, the author and the publisher assume no responsibility for your actions.

Any people depicted in stock imagery provided by Thinkstock are models, and such images are being used for illustrative purposes only.
Certain stock imagery © Thinkstock.

Printed in the United States of America.

ISBN: 978-1-4525-7970-2 (sc)
ISBN: 978-1-4525-7971-9 (e)

Balboa Press rev. date: 8/20/2013

DEDICATION

This booklet is dedicated to all of the members and friends of Unity Church of the Quad Cities in Moline, Illinois who gave me a large number of opportunities to learn about and teach the principles in this booklet!

The time with you was the very best 13 ½ years of my life!

I love, bless and appreciate you ALL!!

INTRODUCTION

The term "NON-VIOLENCE," as used by Gandhi and Martin Luther King and others is very much more than simply the absence of violence! It is the recognition of everything that is good in our lives! This is love, life, peace, health, happiness, right relationships and ALL THINGS GOOD! Furthermore, the main concept that they wanted to reveal was that this goodness is the rightful domain of every person on the planet!

It is the purpose of this booklet to present a thorough understanding of steps that we can all take to make our lives, the lives of those around us and the lives of all persons in the world better through a more thorough understanding and utilization of NON-VIOLENCE.

In this time, there is a lot of energy given to the opposites of NON-VIOLENCE. Our children and adults are bombarded with acts of actual violence in movies and on television, in video games and in newspapers and comic books as well as in all avenues of life. Anger, fear, worry, murder, and who knows what–all are presented to all members of our population as if these are the normal activities of life! Friends, they are NOT! We are here to be happy, healthy, prosperous and successful.

One of my concerns is that people who grow up without family members and others who set a good example of what life can be, will develop their life patterns by what they observe in the movies and on television!

In this booklet, I am making a more thorough understanding of NON-VIOLENCE my contribution to society. My goal is to bring this information to all citizens of our nation and the world. Hopefully, as we all start practicing the techniques that we will read about in this booklet, we will build a consciousness or awareness of NON-VIOLENCE that will help us to create a safer, healthier, and more productive world. I plan to bring this information to churches of all denominations, nursing homes, hospitals, prisons, jails, service clubs and all organizations that will allow me to present a clearer understanding of NON-VIOLENCE and what we can do to bring it forth in our world.

This short booklet may seem to be an "easy read," but I recommend that you see it, not as something to simply read, but something to help change lives! At the end of each section, there is an affirmation that YOU can use to change YOUR consciousness and that can be used to help family members, friends, co-workers and others also do this! My belief, friends, is that NON-VIOLENCE is the result of an inner change that takes place within us!

In her book, "INSTANT HEALING" Dr. Susan Shumsky has the statement, *"Those who understand spiritual principles know that there is only one way for the planet to change: People must change."* (Shumsky p. 189) True NON-VIOLENCE, friends, is NOT the result of building bigger bombs nor acquiring more weapons and building bigger armies, etc. It is the result of an inner change being adopted in all of humanity. This starts with YOU and ME! For this reason, I urge each reader to see the pages that follow for the life changing possibilities that we ALL can develop!

There has been a lot of information in the news in recent years about terrorists, bombers, dictators and bullies, among others. I claim that practicing the suggestions discussed in this booklet will minimize these situations because we will create a consciousness of God's goodness that will improve society so that activities performed by these negative influences will be experienced less and less.

When I use the term, "New Thought" I am referring to a system of thinking which recognizes that we are all one with God and God's goodness as demonstrated by Jesus Christ. Furthermore, "Truth Students" is a general term used for people who are on the path to developing a greater understanding of this thinking.

I have come up with one suggestion or technique that we ALL can follow to create NON-VIOLENCE in every part of our lives for each letter of the alphabet. You will see these presented below in a manner that we can use to make our lives better, the lives of family members better and will ultimately improve the lives of all citizens of all countries on our planet.

 **is for ALWAYS!**

To practice this step, we are to ALWAYS know that we ALL were created in the image and after the likeness of God (Genesis 1:26). So, just as God is ALL things good, so are YOU and I and EVERYONE ELSE all things good. We read in the First Book of John that "God is Love" (1 John 4:16). Based on the premise above, you are love and I am love and everyone else is Love! To live the life of NON-VIOLENCE, then, it is important to know this about ourselves and EVERYBODY in our lives. This is very hard to do for some people that we know, but it is NECESSARY in order to make the improvements to our planet that we are discussing here.

As a matter of fact, troublesome people in our lives are there because they NEED us to know this Truth about them. They probably are not aware of this, but it is important for us to know that they were created in the image and likeness of God as we all were. This is a great step to take to bring more of the attributes of NON-VIOLENCE into our world.

Continuing on our teaching for the letter A, we can know that no one is any better than anyone else! Other people may SEEM superior or inferior to us and we may SEEM superior or inferior to others, but this is just an illusion. Judging others by their skin color, education, country of origin, language, etc. is not the activity of one who practices this teaching. This also helps us comply with the teachings of our Master Teacher, Jesus Christ, who told us to "Do not judge". (Matt 1:1)

Our affirmation for the letter A is:

> FROM THIS DAY FORTH, I PLEDGE TO SEE
> EVERY PERSON IN MY LIFE AS CREATED
> IN THE IMAGE AND AFTER THE LIKENESS
> OF GOD!!

 **is for BROTHER!**

It is MY job and YOUR job and the job of every person in the world to know that we ALL are brothers and sisters to each other!

If every person in the world knew that everybody else was his or her sister or brother, there would surely be fewer and fewer wars and murders, and shootings and killings in our world. We would make it our mission in life to express peace and harmony in every activity!

Jesus told us "This is my commandment, that ye love one another as I have loved you" (John 15:12). He loved all people and treated them equally. This is a GREAT example for us to follow. EVERY person in our lives today is our brother or our sister! EVERY person! As we drive to work or take our children to school or go to lunch or wherever we go today or every day, EVERY person that we encounter will be our brother or sister!

Just think of how you would treat them if they <u>really</u> were your blood relatives! Would you greet them with a smile or a handshake or a hug? Now, I know that we might be arrested if we went about hugging everybody on the street, but, we CAN demonstrate unconditional love toward them in other ways! Following suggestions in this booklet can help us.

I have heard of the rule of 50 which indicates that we ALL have a certain number of people in our lives that we affect in our routine activities. It might be 30 or 50 people or another number, but there always are people who are affected by the way that we think of them or express toward them! And they express toward a certain number of people and each of the people that they encounter affects a certain number of others, etc. Friends, THIS is the key! Our expressions of love toward others CAN be the key to making our world better! My suggestion is to start seeing every person as our brother or sister, and, as we do, THEY will start seeing every person in THEIR lives as their brother or sister and so on and so on and so on! This is a GREAT activity to bring more and more NON-VIOLENCE into our world!

Our Affirmation for B is:

> AS I COMMIT TO LIVING BY THE LAW OF LOVE, I FIND THAT MY LIFE AND MY WORLD GET BETTER AND BETTER!!

 **is for the absence of CUSSWORDS.**

CUSSWORDS, friends, are of the intellect or ego. NON-VIOLENCE is of the Spirit! To grow in NON-VIOLENCE, it is important to see this as a Spiritual activity! We are created to be spiritual persons and as we take time to grow spiritually, we find the REAL us that we were created to be!

Cussing does the opposite! When we participate in this activity, we GROW the human of existence instead of LESSENING it! To make the world better and better, we are to let go of the human and awaken the divinity within ourselves. THAT is what helps us grow in NON-VIOLENCE which will make our lives and our world better.

The ego world, of which we are a part, is growing in use of CUSSWORDS and it appears that this is becoming a part of everyday activities in almost every part of life! This is where YOU and I come in! We do not have to use these. Especially when we see that they make our world <u>worse</u> instead of better! When we use these, we are n<u>ot</u> expanding the use of NON-VIOLENCE, we are simply making the opposite more and more prevalent!

Our affirmation for this is:

> AS MY GOAL IS TO MAKE MY LIFE AND
> OUR WORLD BETTER, I VOW FROM THIS
> DAY FORTH TO MINIMIZE MY USE OF
> CUSSWORDS.

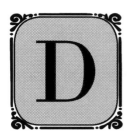 **is for DIVINE ORDER.**

DIVINE ORDER can be defined as the perfection that our earth and everything and everyone on it was created to experience. This includes: peace, love, harmony, joy, prosperity and all of God's goodness for ALL of us. We can easily see that NON-VIOLENCE is certainly a part of DIVINE ORDER.

If we do not experience the fullness of Divine Order that we were created to experience, it may be because we have "bought into" the untruth that we are "only" human beings. We are NOT only human beings. Jesus taught that we are Spiritual Beings on the planet living in these human bodies. It is our mission to demonstrate the Goodness of Life that God has for us to experience! This is finding the Divine Order that is ours by being expressions of Spirit.

To find more and more DIVINE ORDER and NON-VIOLENCE in our lives, try a technique that is used by Truth Students: start each day with prayer and meditation and by affirming "DIVINE ORDER" and then repeat the phrase several times during the day. This helps our consciousness awaken to the Truth of Life that we are on the planet to experience, which, of course, includes all of the attributes of NON-VIOLENCE.

DIVINE ORDER is the basic right of every person on our planet. Of course, this includes NON-VIOLENCE as well. It is our job to remember this for ourselves, for friends, family members, and for all people everywhere!

Our affirmation for this is:

> AS I SPEND MORE TIME IN PRAYER AND MEDITATION, SO DO I FIND MORE AND MORE DIVINE ORDER IN MY LIFE AND SO DO I FIND MORE AND MORE PEACE AND HAPPINESS.

 **is for ENERGY.**

When we are energetic as a result of God's presence in our lives, we find the perfection, joy, harmony and goodness that are ours to experience. This builds an invisible shield around us that only allows God's goodness into our lives. As this occurs, we find all of the attributes of NON-VIOLENCE.

It is important to recognize that we ALL have ALL of the energy in us that we will ever need! As we take the time to call upon it and channel it into bringing more NON-VIOLENCE into our world, so will this happen!

It is also important to recognize that we have a choice of how we will use our energy. We can bring forth more of God's goodness into our world, or we can use it to create more negativity. As we start our day with prayer and meditation and by following other suggestions in this booklet we will find the abundance of God's goodness that we were created to experience!

The other important point is to know that all others have this ability as well. As we see them developing this awareness, it will help their lives improve as well.

Our affirmation for this is:

> I HAVE ALL OF THE ENERGY THAT I
> NEED TO BRING MORE AND MORE NON-
> VIOLENCE INTO MY WORLD!

 **is for FORGIVENESS.**

In the Lord's Prayer, Jesus told us that we are forgiven as we forgive. Because unforgiveness is a blockage to our good, practicing FORGIVENESS opens us to the love, peace, health and other forms of NON-VIOLENCE that are ours by Divine right. God cannot hold any unforgiveness toward us because God is Love. As we recognize this and recognize that we are God's Image and Likeness, we become aware that we are Love as well! Therefore, when we express unforgiveness toward ourselves or anyone else, we are not expressing our full and complete nature.

Because we are Spiritual Beings, FORGIVENESS is one of our natural characteristics. As we recognize and let go of the concept that we are "only human" so do we find that expressing FORGIVENESS becomes easier and easier.

A good practice is to recite a FORGIVENESS statement similar to the affirmation on the following page every day, say, at bedtime. After reciting, wait to see if any names come that want to be included with your statement. Do the statement for them and then see if other names come. Continue this until no further names appear.

Our affirmation for FORGIVENESS is:

GOD LOVES, BLESSES, APPRECIATES AND
FORGIVES ME, I LOVE, BLESS, APPRECIATE
AND FORGIVE ME AND I LOVE, BLESS,
APPRECIATE AND FORGIVE ALL PEOPLE
IN MY LIFE!

 is for **GOD'S GRACE.**

GOD'S GRACE has been defined as the goodness of God that is available to ALL of us whether we think we deserve it or not! This applies to our "enemies" as well as to us and our friends and family members! I have put the word, "enemies" in quotation marks because it is my view that we have no "enemies" except in our minds. This definition comes from accepting and living the teachings that are being presented in this booklet.

Our job, as promoters of NON-VIOLENCE, is to recognize that God loves us and everybody in our lives equally! We can use this as a precedent and love everybody in our lives as well. God, being Love, doesn't see the "stuff." God sees through eyes of love, only seeing goodness in all people, everywhere.

Many people have not been taught to follow God's example. They are caught up in what they see with their human eyes, read in the newspapers, see on television and hear from others, etc., and seeing through the eyes of love is very foreign to them.

To bring more NON-VIOLENCE into our lives and theirs, we can start out our day by accepting GOD'S GRACE and recognizing that this applies to all people in our lives equally. This can be a major step to bringing NON-VIOLENCE into our lives and into our world.

Our affirmation for G is:

> THANK YOU, GOD FOR YOUR GRACE THAT IS MAKING MY LIFE AND THE LIVES OF ALL PEOPLE EVERYWHERE BETTER AND BETTER!

 **is for HARMONY.**

HARMONY has a definition in New Thought, just as it does in music. In New Thought, it is thought of as "perfect accord with the goodness, the beauty and the righteousness of omnipresent Spirit" (Revealing Word" p. 91).

When we are in harmony in our relationships, we are experiencing the divine goodness that Spirit has for us to enjoy. As we start out our day saying to ourselves that we are on this planet to live in harmony and peace, we set ourselves in tune with the goodness that God has for us to experience and we find that our relationships get better and better. My mother used to say that "it takes two to tangle," which reminds me that we can keep all of our relationships harmonious by starting out each day by saying to ourselves: "today, I am experiencing perfect peace. THANK YOU, GOD!"

When we do this, we build a consciousness of NON-VIOLENCE that will keep anger, fear, worry and their corresponding activities from being expressed in our lives and in our world!

This would bring NON-VIOLENCE into our lives, into the lives of those that are around us and all of our world.

Our affirmation for this is:

> IT IS MY NATURE TO BE HARMONIOUS
> AND HAPPY. AS I START OUT MY
> DAY FOCUSED ON The WONDERFUL
> ATTRIBUTES OF NON-VIOLENCE, I FIND
> PEACE, LOVE, HEALTH AND HAPPINESS IN
> EVERY ACTIVITY.

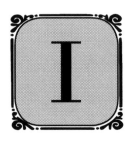 **is for IMAGINATION**

IMAGINATION is a very important activity in New Thought: a belief that we can become what we see ourselves experiencing. As we visualize ourselves living the activities of NON-VIOLENCE, we find that they start to appear! This is a means by which we can create or at least control our environments! As we take time to see ourselves experiencing the goodness of life that goes with NON-VIOLENCE, we find it in every part of our lives! Love and Health and Wholeness and Right and Perfect Relationships are created in our minds first, through our IMAGINATIONS: Then, they appear in our lives!

It is my experience that people generally are not aware of the magnificent power that we can get out of our IMAGINATIONS. We do not take time to focus on the potential goodness that is available, instead, by default, we focus on the examples that are set for us on television, in the movies, etc. In most cases, these step away from the fullness of the <u>real</u> goodness that we were created to experience. As we take time to focus our energies on the divine goodness that is available to us all, we find the magnificent NON-VIOLENCE that can make our lives and our world better.

We can also use our IMAGINATIONS to see family members and friends and all others experiencing the fullness of NON-VIOLENCE that are on the planet for us all to experience.

Our affirmation for IMAGINATION is:

> AS I TAKE THE TIME DAILY TO SEE MYSELF EXPERIENCING THE FULLNESS OF NON-VIOLENCE, MY LIFE AND MY WORLD BECOME BETTER AND BETTER!

 **is for JUDGMENT**

JUDGMENT

Our Master Teacher, Jesus Christ, told us "Do not judge, so that you may not be judged" (Matt. 7:1). He also told us to ". . . judge with right judgment" (John 7:24). By these two statements, He was telling us to see everybody in our life experience as the perfect expressions of God that they were created to be! I like to say we should "see them as God sees them". This is important, for God is Love, and God sees us all as His children. God loves us all because of this and it is important to know this for ourselves and for all others in our relationships.

The most important person that we should practice this with, of course, is ourselves! If we see ourselves as the wonderful expressions of God that we have been created to be, we will find the right and perfect answers for every part of our lives! When we live in this manner each day, it becomes easier and easier to see others through the eyes of Love as we were intended to do.

My biggest problem with this is with drivers! The very day that I was putting this together: When I went to lunch, first,

I encountered a man that didn't stop at a stop sign and turned right in front of me. Next, when I came to a four way stop, I stopped to wait until my turn came, and someone didn't wait for his turn and pulled out right in front of me. Lastly, I had a young lady follow me very closely (approximately 5 feet away from my back bumper) for about 8 blocks until she finally turned. I was going exactly the speed limit, but she must have wanted to go faster! In each case, I reminded myself of this lesson and kept repeating: "YOU ARE A PERFECT EXPRESSION OF GOD!" "YOU ARE A PERFECT EXPRESSION OF GOD!" "YOU ARE A PERFECT EXPRESSION OF GOD!" I am sure that these conditions were to remind me that I DO have some growing to do in the arena of NON-VIOLENCE.

Our affirmation for JUDGMENT is:

I AM MAKING IT MY RESPONSIBILITY NOW TO "JUDGE RIGHTEOUS JUDGMENT." AS I DO THIS, I AM DOING MY PART TO MAKE THIS WORLD MORE AND MORE NON-VIOLENT!

 **is for KINDNESS**

KINDNESS is to me, a very important part of living a NON-VIOLENT life!

It can be very simple to fairly complicated, but it is VERY IMPORTANT to living the fullness of NON-VIOLENCE that we are created to experience. From opening the door for another to sharing your home with them and all kinds of things in between.

As we think of ourselves and all others as created in the Image and Likeness of God, it becomes easier and easier to share kindness. We can start by knowing how much the Creator loves, blesses and appreciates us. When we look at the earth and see its many benefits: the magnificent topsoil for growing our food, the fantastic air with just the right proportions of oxygen that our bodies need to survive, the abundant supply of water that is necessary for our existence, etc. It is AMAZING how much God loves, blesses and appreciates us and shows kindness to us in ALL of this wonderful goodness.

As we realize how much God loves us, we can express more KINDNESS toward ourselves and build on this to develop the ability to express more and more KINDNESS toward all others in our lives.

It was reported that the older brother of the two young men who were implicated in the bombings in Boston recently told the authorities that he had lived in this country for ten years and had no friends from the U.S. I want to point out that things might have been quite different if someone would have approached him with KINDNESS during that ten year period.

My affirmation for KINDNESS is:

> I AM ON THIS PLANET TO DO GOOD AND TO BE KIND TO EVERYBODY IN MY LIFE. I CHOOSE TO DO THAT TODAY AND EVERY DAY!

 **is for unconditional LOVE!**

It is easy to understand that unconditional LOVE and NON-VIOLENCE are intertwined. When we have LOVE in our hearts, there is absolutely no room for any of the opposites of NON-VIOLENCE. One of the statements that we have from Jesus is "Just as I have loved you, you also shall love one another" (John 13:34).

Jesus KNEW that God is Love and He wanted us to realize that as well. Because of this, He expressed unconditional love to all persons in His life. You may recall that, when He was asked for help, He gave help, in many forms. He healed the sick, fed thousands of people, cured the blind and the deaf, and did many other things to help people without asking them what religion they were, or what nationality or any other questions. He just HELPED them unconditionally!

As we follow this example, we find that our world becomes more loving and cooperative and we bring this unconditional LOVE forth into the awareness of others in our lives.

There are numerous ways that we can demonstrate unconditional LOVE toward others, and I urge each reader of this booklet to find the right and perfect methods for each situation in his or her life.

Our affirmation for unconditional LOVE is:

GOD IS LOVE, I AM LOVE. I SPREAD LOVE WHEREVER I GO!

 **is for MOOD.**

There is a major problem in this world today in that people do not realize that THEY are in charge of their moods and can change them if they choose to! You hear people say, "I woke up this morning in a bad mood." or "What you said to me made me feel bad," etc. It is important to recognize that WE can change our moods at any time!

We often hear people say: "she made me do it" or "they made me do it," etc. and it is important to know that NO ONE can make us do anything! NO ONE! For WE are in charge of our own actions!

The important thing about this is that OUR moods can affect the moods of others who don't know that they have this control.

Because of this, taking charge of our own moods can be a life changer for, not only us, but for EVERY PERSON in our lives! This is because our moods affect others in our lives, including family members, co-workers and many others. So, taking charge of our moods can be a GREAT ACTIVITY that we all can use to bring more NON-VIOLENCE into our lives and into our world.

Our affirmation for M is:

> TODAY IS THE FIRST DAY OF THE REST OF MY LIFE. I CHOOSE TO NOT LET ANYTHING DISTURB MY LIFE BY HOLDING TO A POSITIVE MOOD IN EVERY ACTIVITY!

is for the NEVER-ENDING Spirit of GOD!

We know from the teachings of Jesus that God is everywhere. Also that God is Love and Peace and all things good. Therefore, we can see that Love and Peace and all of God's goodness are everywhere as well! To see God everywhere can help us grow in greater awareness of the magnificence of NON-VIOLENCE. Daily prayer and meditation help us become more aware of Goodness and this brings more and more NON-VIOLENCE into our lives and into the world!

As we have stated, God is everywhere, in everything, and the omnipresence of NON-VIOLENCE becomes more and more visible as we start our day by recalling that God's goodness is everywhere we go!

This is what our Master Teacher, Jesus Christ was telling us when He said, "Do not judge by appearances but judge with right judgment" (John 7:24) He was reminding us that God is everywhere, in everything and it is our responsibility to see this Presence in every person, situation and activity in our lives.

It may be difficult to do this for some people, situations and activities, but it is VERY important! Hitler, for instance, was created in the image and likeness of God just as you and I were, but during his early years, this teaching was not reinforced in his consciousness. It is my contention that he could have used his talents to make the world better if he would have been brought up in an atmosphere that kept him aware of this.

If he had people in his life who practiced the principles in this booklet, who knows what Europe would be like today?

Our affirmation for this is:

> AS I AWAKEN TO THE MAGNIFICENT PRESENCE OF GOD THAT IS WITHIN ME AND ALL AROUND ME, I FIND MORE AND MORE NON-VIOLENCE IN EVERY PART OF MY WORLD!!

 **is for ONENESS!!**

As we recognize that we are ONE with everybody and everything in the world, so do we find it easier and easier to be open to NON-VIOLENCE! When we know that we are ONE with everybody and everything, we find that it is easier to demonstrate the magnificent characteristics that are part of NON-VIOLENCE which includes the goodness of God: Peace, Love and Happiness that can make our world so much better and better.

As it has been stated, we are brothers and sisters with all people everywhere and this awareness can bring us to an existence where there are no wars, no shootings, no murders or robberies or other situations of violence.

If we know that God is love, peace, harmony and all things good and that you and I and all people everywhere are one with God, so are we one with all of this ever-present goodness. Practicing the suggestions in this booklet will help us and all others develop the awareness to have God's goodness, including NON-VIOLENCE, available to all.

This may not happen in our lifetime, but as we continue to practice these teachings and pass them on to friends, family members and all friends everywhere, it WILL HAPPEN!

Our affirmation for ONENESS is:

> I AM ONE WITH GOD, ONE WITH JESUS AND ONE WITH EVERYBODY AND EVERYTHING THAT EXISTS. AS I BECOME MORE AND MORE AWARE OF THIS, I FIND THE GOODNESS OF NON-VIOLENCE IN EVERY ACTIVITY! THANK YOU, GOD!

is for PEACE

PEACE is a very important part of NON-VIOLENCE. In New Thought, we teach that true PEACE is not something that we acquire from outside of ourselves. In the world, it is taught that we can make peace by acquiring more weapons or building stronger bombs or by creating bigger armies, etc. but in New Thought, we feel that this type of peace is fleeting at best. REAL PEACE comes from within us. As we spend time daily in the Quiet, we "tune in" to the PEACE of God that is within us. Therefore, we find God's NON-VIOLENCE in every activity. This helps us to get along with all persons in our lives.

To us, the key to a stronger, longer lasting PEACE in the world is to develop NON-VIOLENCE through the activities that are discussed in this booklet. We like to say that PEACE is available to all persons everywhere! As we become more aware of God within us through prayer and meditation, we develop more PEACE and more and more NON-VIOLENCE that we are able to express in our every activity!

We learn that PEACE is truly an inside job! Focusing on God within helps us find the right and perfect answers in every part of our lives and this includes PEACE and all of the other attributes of NON-VIOLENCE.

Our affirmation for Peace is:

> PEACE and NON-VIOLENCE ARE THE RESULTS OF DOING MY INNER WORK. I PROPOSE TO FOLLOW THESE TEACHINGS EVERY DAY TO HELP MY LIFE, MY RELATIONSHIPS AND MY WORLD!

 **is for QUALITY**

QUALITY is a very important part of NON-VIOLENCE. As we visualize ourselves expressing a QUALITY life, we find that we are expressing the goodness of NON-VIOLENCE that we are here to enjoy. We quiet down our minds and focus on the characteristics of NON-VIOLENCE that we wish to experience, and we find that they become a part of our daily lives!

We have heard of the phrase "Quality Time." This usually refers to parents participating in activities with their children that will involve enjoyable interaction between them. But, it can also apply to other relationships as well. Husbands and wives, brothers and sisters and ALL people in our lives. Our relationships with ALL people in our lives can be enhanced by committing to experience "Quality Time" with them.

I heard a story on Public Radio about this recently:

> A young boy approached his grandfather and asked
> him if he loved him. The grandfather responded by
> telling him that he loved him very much and asked
> what brought this up.

The boy responded by telling him that he sometimes could not feel the love when his grandfather was not paying attention to him.

As we commit ourselves to spending quality time with all others in our lives, we experience more of the goodness of NON-VIOLENCE and we make our world better!

Our affirmation for this is:

> AS I FOCUS ON THE QUALITY OF LIFE THAT IS MINE TO EXPERIENCE, IT HAPPENS AND I BRING MORE NON-VIOLENCE INTO MY WORLD.

 **is for REALITY**

In New Thought, REALITY has two very different definitions. We like to say that there is "Reality" which is God's plan for our lives and "reality" which is the existence of life we are experiencing currently. In "Reality," we have available the fullness of God's goodness that we were created to enjoy. This includes Life and Love and Peace and Harmony and all the characteristics of NON-VIOLENCE all the time!

The "reality" is that which we are currently experiencing. This may include more human activities, and can have some of the qualities that are opposite to those that we associate with NON-VIOLENCE. As we make it our goal to bring our level of reality up to our desired level of Reality, we achieve the levels of the characteristics of NON-VIOLENCE that will make our lives and our world better!

This comes from following the suggestions in this booklet and from practicing daily prayer and meditation.

It is a commitment that will have great rewards in bringing NON-VIOLENCE into our lives and into our world.

Our affirmation for REALITY is:

> GOD'S PLAN FOR MY LIFE IS TO
> EXPERIENCE NON-VIOLENCE IN EVERY
> ACTIVITY. AS I MAKE IT MY GOAL TO
> EXPERIENCE THIS, IT HAPPENS!

 **is for Self-Esteem.**

I am not a psychologist nor a psychiatrist, but I am willing to bet that every terrorist, every bomb-builder and even every bully on our planet is suffering from low self-esteem.

This also applies, in one degree or another, to every one of us who is going through any sort of a personal problem. "He doesn't love me anymore" or "she doesn't love me" or problems with co-workers or even financial difficulties. These are simply the results of not knowing the Truth about ourselves.

In New Thought, the answer to low Self-Esteem is found in the teachings of the Bible. In the Old Testament, we read that all mankind was created in the Image and after the Likeness of God (Genesis 1:26). I claim that very few members of the human race are aware of this teaching, or at best, are aware of the magnificent meaning of this!

We have mentioned before that God is good and that, being created in the image and likeness of God makes us good as well! But very few of us, to my knowledge anyway, understand the meaning that this can have for our lives.

Jesus wanted all persons in the world to know this wonderful Truth. His statement "AND YOU WILL KNOW THE TRUTH AND THE TRUTH WILL MAKE YOU FREE" (John 8:32), was meant to inform us of this.

As we learn this Truth about ourselves, so do we find that we can know and live it about all others in our lives as well.

As we start practicing this Truth for ourselves, it becomes easier and easier to know it for others. Then, we will be on the path to bringing more and more NON-VIOLENCE into our world.

Our affirmation for this is:

> I WAS CREATED IN THE IMAGE AND LIKENESS OF GOD AND SO WAS EVERYONE ELSE.

 **Is for THANK YOU, GOD!!**

As we express Gratitude to God for the Good that we have in our lives, for the peace, health, harmony and NON-VIOLENCE, so do we find that this brings MORE of God's goodness into our awareness.

So, it is recommended that we ALL take time daily to express THANKS to GOD for ALL of the goodness that we are experiencing.

We express Gratitude for our food before each meal, but what about expressing Gratitude for the fresh air, for the sunshine, for the rabbits and ducks and geese and what about our friends and family members and what about the trees and bushes and roads and highways and gasoline and our transportation devices and computers and homes and offices, etc.

Being Grateful can help us find the magnificent goodness of God that we are here to experience, and, friends, that DOES include NON-VIOLENCE!

Also, gratitude works very effectively to help us accomplish our goals. Being grateful before we achieve them is helpful, I think, because it helps us raise our consciousness and this opens us to receive more and more good.

It is also important to know that gratitude also helps that which we are grateful for to grow in our lives. As we say THANK YOU, GOD for the attributes of NON-VIOLENCE that we are experiencing, we find more and more of them! Being grateful for the attributes of NON-VIOLENCE may appear to be a small step, but it can be a very important one to help our world improve!!

Our affirmation for THANK YOU is:

> THANK YOU, GOD, FOR BRINGING YOUR GOODNESS, INCLUDING NON-VIOLENCE INTO EVERY AREA OF MY LIFE AND OUR WORLD!

 **is for UNDERSTANDING.**

If there ever is a problem in our world, it could be that we have not listened to or tried to understand those people in our lives! We have heard that this is a major problem between husbands and wives in today's society. If we do not listen to and make an attempt to UNDERSTAND our spouses, how much do you think that we listen to and UNDERSTAND others?

It can easily be seen that listening and UNDERSTANDING are very important to bringing NONVIOLENCE into our lives and into our world. In our families, it is important to turn off the television or at least turn the sound down and LISTEN to what the person has to say. It IS important or he/she would not be saying it!

In our busy world today, it DOES take commitment to be willing to try to understand persons in our lives! If we are living by the Law of Love as we have discussed previously, we certainly can take the time to give each person time to tell us what is on his or her mind.

A shortened definition of UNDERSTANDING is "to see God standing under all things and people." If we see God in all people, we can recognize that they DO have something valuable to say.

So, to commit to REALLY listening to all persons in our experience is a GREAT step to bringing more NON-VIOLENCE into our world.

Another facet of UNDERSTANDING is our ability to listen to God. We call this meditation. As we quiet our minds and bodies to listen, we receive the right and perfect ideas to make our lives and our world better. We might not hear words at the time, but as time proceeds we will be guided to take the right steps to do this. This applies to every facet of life, including all of the attributes of NON-VIOLENCE.

Our affirmation for this is:

AS MY INTENTION IS TO MAKE THE WORLD BETTER, I COMMIT TO BECOMING A BETTER LISTENER!

 **is for VOLUNTEERING.**

VOLUNTEERING is an activity that can draw every segment of society together! When we volunteer to help others, we are doing what Jesus said when He told us. "Truly, I tell you, just as you did it to the least of these, who are members of my family, you did it to me" (Matt. 25:40).

We have said before that much of our definition of violence is a result of not listening to others with understanding. When we VOLUNTEER to help others, we are giving ourselves and others the opportunity to listen to and learn about each other! In doing that, we train ourselves to see that the other people are indeed much more than members of the group that we have come to help or to work with. They are individualized expressions of God! AND, they begin to see the very same about us!

This can be a GREAT activity to bring more NON-VIOLENCE into our world!

There are volunteer opportunities everywhere: In our community, there are walks for cancer, for heart disease, for mental illness and for many others of the troubles that are being experienced in our country. Participating in these or bicycle rides or other activities are a means of showing others that you care and are helping to raise awareness or funds or other necessities to help make our world better! Some folks participate in Habitat for Humanity to help build homes for people who are less fortunate, work at food pantries, help at senior citizen centers, serve as teaching assistants for schools or teach English as a second language in locations where this is needed. There are many areas of life where we all can volunteer to help make our world better. I have belonged to a Befriender's group for one of the local hospitals where we would visit residents to help them feel better.

Also, giving blood is a way of volunteering to make our world better. I was very excited recently when I saw that our local blood center had sent 100 units of blood to the hospitals in Boston where the people that were injured by the bombing were being helped. WOW! To have my blood being used in this very dramatic situation makes me a hero! I CAN help in situations that are difficult! There are many other ways in which we can contribute to making our world better. Let us all start seeing ourselves as VOLUNTEERS who are helping to bring more and more NON-VIOLENCE into our world!

Our affirmation for this is:

> BECAUSE I WANT TO SEE MORE AND MORE AND MORE NON-VIOLENCE IN MY WORLD, I AM COMMITTED TO VOLUN-TEERING WHENEVER POSSIBLE!

 **is for WE!**

WE are the vehicles that can bring NON-VIOLENCE into our world. As a matter of fact, WE are the ONLY vehicles that can do it! The lions and tigers cannot do it, the elephants cannot do it and the tulips and roses and trees and bushes cannot do it. It is up to us!

I urge each reader of this booklet to read through it again, this time, asking ourselves what WE can do, or more specifically, "What can I do to bring more NON-VIOLENCE into our world?"

I have just "tipped the bucket" of what can be done. WE are on the cusp of bringing more NON-VIOLENCE into our world and each person on our planet, whether they read this or not, has the opportunity to participate in it.

So, as we have discussed before, each of us has the opportunity to do our part and to encourage friends, neighbors, relatives and all others to also do their part! As each of us commits to helping accomplish this, we find that our world is indeed getting better and better!

A good idea is to ask ourselves in meditation what we can do to help bring this about. Another is to commit each day, upon awakening, to doing what can be done to bring more NON-VIOLENCE into our world.

Our affirmation for this is:

> AS AN INDIVIDUALIZED EXPRESSION OF GOD, I HAVE A VERY IMPORTANT MISSION, THAT OF BRINGING MORE NON-VIOLENCE INTO OUR WORLD!

is for EXAMPLE!

Whether we know it or not or whether people in our lives are aware of it, we are always setting an EXAMPLE for others around us. This activity involves the Law of 50(or 30) as described earlier.

This makes every step that we make in the name of NON-VIOLENCE a multi-faceted activity! We not only are taking a step to make our world better, but we are setting examples that others may follow to do this as well!!

A while back, I went into the pizza shop where my grandson works to see him about something. When I was leaving, there was a lady behind me with two young girls who was carrying several pizza boxes. So, as I went out of the store, I held the door for her and her daughters to get out. There was a young man following her, so I held the door for him as well. He made the statement, "Oh, you don't have to hold it for me," but I did anyway. Then, the woman had to walk between two cars with her daughters and her pizza and open the door for the girls to get into the car. The young man saw that there was a logistics problem for the woman, so he hurried ahead and helped her with the girls and the door and the pizza, saying, "Here, let me help." Of course, I cannot prove that his kindness was a result of my kindness toward him, but my response is, "You cannot prove that it wasn't."

The thing is that kindness is "creative." You and I may not ever know of the full results of the actions that we take, but, we can know that "GOOD BEGETS GOOD."

We only need to turn to the 4 gospels to see that Jesus was kind and loving toward all persons that He encountered. As we follow the EXAMPLES that He set, we will continue the process of bringing more and more NON-VIOLENCE into our world.

Our affirmation for this is:

> BECAUSE I AM COMMITTED TO MAKING MY WORLD BETTER, I AGREE TO TAKE ACTIONS THAT WILL SET A GOOD EXAMPLE FOR OTHERS TO FOLLOW!

 **is for YOUR WORLD.**

This world belongs to YOU and ME and ALL the other approximately 7 billion humans on the planet! We cannot be responsible for what the other 6.99999999999999 billion or so people do to make it better, but, we ARE responsible for OUR actions! As we commit to living the suggestions in this booklet, we WILL be doing our part to help bring forth more and more NON-VIOLENCE into our existence and the existence of all others in the world!

When we first wake up in the morning, we can ask ourselves, "What is it that I can do today to make my world better?" The answers may not appear immediately, but as you proceed on your day, ideas WILL appear to help bring more NON-VIOLENCE into our existence!

To follow this suggestion, I have slightly modified one of my favorite statements. For this purpose, it is:

God loves, blesses and appreciates me,
I love bless and appreciate me,
I love, bless and appreciate everybody and everything in my world!

As we work with this statement, we will convince our consciousness of the Truth of our existence.

Our affirmation for Y is:

I AM COMMITTED TO DOING WHAT I CAN DO TO BRING MORE NON-VIOLENCE INTO MY WORLD!

 **is for ZEAL and ENTHUSIASM!!**

In his book, "The REVEALING WORD", Charles Fillmore, Co-Founder of the Unity School of Christianity, defines ZEAL as "Intensity, ardor, enthusiasm . . . the mighty force that incites the winds, the tides, the storms; it urges the planet on its course and spurs the ant to greater exertion . . ."(Revealing Word p.216)

I am asking each reader of this little booklet to get ZEALOUS and ENTHUSIASTIC about NON-VIOLENCE! If each of us does "our part" we will be a major impetus that will bring more love and peace and harmony into our world!

Whatever our position in life is, be it a schoolteacher, a bus driver, a policeman or retired or whatever, we CAN make our world better through practicing the teachings of NON-VIOLENCE!

As we get ZEALOUS about practicing these principles, so we will find, slowly, but surely, that our world is becoming a better expression of the goodness that we have been taught is possible!

Some readers may not know that the word, "enthusiastic" comes from the Greek, "EN THEOS" which means "in God". As we recognize that we are "in God" and God is "in us" we cannot not get enthusiastic about our lives and the accomplishment of the goals that we have set.

Enthusiasm, as some of the other qualities in this booklet, is "catching." As you and I get more and more enthusiastic about bringing more and more NON-VIOLENCE into our world, so does it pass on to others! All readers are invited to join me in getting enthusiastic about making these changes in our world!

Our affirmation for ZEAL is:

I AM EXCITED AND ENTHUSIASTIC ABOUT CHANGING MY WORLD THROUGH PRACTICING THE PRINCIPLES OF NON-VIOLENCE!!

CLOSING

It is my purpose in this booklet to get readers to recognize that they have the capabilities, the opportunities and the responsibility to help bring more and more NON-VIOLENCE into our world.

As mentioned above, as each of us does this, we WILL create a world that has more love, peace, harmony and goodness in it.

Thank you very much for helping!

Rev. Dean

JUST REACH OUT
Jan Mahannah

BOOKS CITED

Fillmore, Charles. <u>The Revealing Word</u> 1959 Unity Village, MO. Unity School of Christianity, 1989

<u>NEW OXFORD ANNOTATED BIBLE with the Apocrypha,</u> New Revised Standard Version, Oxford University Press, 1989

Shumsky, Susan. <u>Instant Healing. Pompton Plains, NJ Career Press, 2013</u>